To Let
Myself Go

To Let Myself Go

Kimberly Olivera Lainez

atmosphere press

"I have rebuilt the ruined places and replanted that which was desolate."

– Ezekiel 36:36

To my Creator, You are my strength, my comfort, everything. For my husband, every word of love is written for you. Thank you for listening to me read countless poem after poem and for being an endless support system. For my readers, I hope that these pages remind you that you are not alone. Though our experiences are individual, we are all experiencing the various seasons and waves of life and are therefore collectively united. I pray that you find something relatable and encouraging among these pages, that you enjoy them (preferably with a big cup of coffee in hand and some sunlight), and that this book can help you the way it's helped me.

Table of Contents

II. Love

III. Sunlight

Unraveling

To Let Myself Go

Teach me the ways of life.

Not the surface, but the root.

Not the shadow, but the essence.

Not the lowly ground, but the sky.

The breaking the sprouting the blooming the glowing

the wicked the lovely the terrible the wonderful

the mourning the dancing the holy.

Take me to the rock that is higher than I.

Strip the immaterial.

Teach me to let myself go.

Sunday Afternoon

The sunset blends into a deep blue.

I hear the distant sounds of cars on the street.

I am lost in my mind.

The clock is ticking in the background,

polished, glass, keeper of time.

We are all, at times, chained to our sorrows.

There is a stillness to this house,

unbothered by the proximity of the rustling trees.

My life is a kaleidoscope of dreams and fears.

Sometimes a withered tree

a soft petal

or a star.

Time is a teasing illusionist.

Night descends to swallow us whole.

Light the Match

You sit at the bottom of the pond

with your heart outside your body,

your heart crushed in your hand,

a red sea of disappointment.

You look into the blue of twilight

and exhale your past

like fog fading into the day.

There is no room for that here.

There is only room for

learning to love yourself again

to forgive

to pray.

You light a match

and set fire to yesterday,

burning the pain like an orange sun,

like a blood red moon

that will be gone

by tomorrow.

Seeker

Often I search for answers

peering into the dark blue dusk

of the world,

the flower of my heart open

waiting in the palm of the dark.

Call it curious call it lost

call it the song of my soul

seeking its missing puzzle piece

in the form of a matching melody

in the form of a question.

Hands outstretched

sky vast and mysterious

here I am

waiting for something holy.

The Stone

Some withered days

your bones are too heavy

to carry

muscles not like your own

your body betrays you.

You lay down,

try to remember how to breathe.

You are so tired.

The stone you swallowed,

the one sitting at the bottom of your stomach

sinking you like an anchor

like a broken thing,

is heavier than you remembered.

I once wished the sun would kiss me

and fill me such overwhelming warmth,

so much warmth I forgot the stone.

Set it down,

you were never meant to carry it.

Last night I dreamt God kissed my face

and I gave him my stubborn heart

in exchange for the stone.

Un-Naming

Un-naming every bad habit

slowly forming the words

bitter and tasteless

slipping out into the drain

swirling away into oblivion.

Rewind, unravel, video child.

Walking backwards

shedding my petals

dripping stains onto the carpet.

If only I'd done this sooner.

I'm done running.

I know the way back home.

Shifting position

changing gears

into forward

into now.

I'll wait for me.

Evening

The evening throws its nets

around your beating heart

and squeezes.

Sometimes you are overflowing

with everything.

The evening fishes for words,

but they have tumbled out of your mouth

onto the ground,

patches of flowers among the field

where they have fallen.

The sun stretches and descends

beyond the hills,

painting the blue in splashes

of gold and orange,

and I cannot step out of my heart.

Instead I am filled with nostalgia

or sadness

or admiration

or some pulling feeling I cannot explain,

and I feel the immensity of my soul

under the immensity of the sky.

Sleepless Heart

Tonight the stars are

weeping your fragrance

and I,

lovestruck and lovesick

before the wild luminescent moon,

howled your name into the night,

bitter and lost within

the valleys of my heart.

The Fog

The fog drapes over the morning

like a white sheet,

like a cloudy curtain

bringing in the

damp musky scent

of the earth.

I grab fistfuls in my hands

and breathe

to mark that I am here,

that I am alive.

I have been filled with

feathered dreams

and drowsy thoughts,

weighed down like thick mud.

The pearly veil vanishes,

fades into the open sky,

and that otherworldly feeling with it,

leaving me with my open heart

in my delicate hands.

At Night

There are things

best kept at night

like the shadow of a kiss

like the secrets of the heart

like a silver sliver of moon

kept in your pocket for safekeeping.

There are different thoughts

like different marbles

smooth and dark

that dance around

and dare to come out

at night

at night

the cricket sings

its lilac song of summer blues

as the dark bleeds into the morning.

At night

your phantom fragrance

fills me with nostalgia

and I am left with thirst

for a cup of you.

Misplaced Dream

I find you in the silence

in the moment between breaths,

silvery and pale,

a lost dream I misplaced

far from my reach

like scattered stars in the night.

I never stop

missing you.

Blue

My favorite time of day

is when the earth is blue

just before the night sweeps in

with its dark coats and stars.

A velvety blue quietly fills the land

in a silent magic that seems to

cover the land in a perpetual dream state.

There is a sense of wonder

a gentle time of reflection

where thoughts tumble out of

their secret box to breathe freely

for a moment.

In the heartbeat of

wild things running free

I am both moved

and lost.

A Night in New York

It's cold in New York tonight

and the stars are brimming

with melancholy,

but that's just a memory

because you can't see the stars here.

Instead the city lights gleam

among the hustle and bustle,

gleam with loss

and yearning

and regret.

I like where I live,

but I don't know if I like

who I've become.

Should I not have traded my soul

for ambition?

You're like a ghost

haunting the vessel

of my depressed mind.

I haven't spoken a word since we parted.

If only I could look upon

the stars and breathe freely

instead of this polluted air

and crowded subway lines,

dirty with all our sins.

I think then I would

let myself unravel,

my eyes soft with sorrow

and tears

and madness,

the madness that comes

with being lonely.

My heart would break loose

into the night sky,

scattered with the wind.

A Stone or a Rose

I shake and shed

the petals of grief.

Sometimes my soul is distant

and quiet.

My thoughts travel like

a river

or the wind,

constantly changing direction,

flowing this way and that,

silky strings of melancholy

like tall blades of grass.

They march on like car wheels

or the seasons

or life.

But sometimes my soul is

full of laughter,

of bouncing energy,

of sunlight

of maddening joy,

of hope,

like branches reaching higher,

like sunflowers meeting the warmth,

letting the sun kiss their faces.

I never know which days

my soul will awaken

a stone

or a rose.

Ready

We gather the pieces scattered–

a little pain there

a little joy here,

the remnants of the year

displayed in my hands

like fragments of a sentence.

My flower heart pours it out,

a river of collected moments

strengthening and teaching

leading me to the next chapter.

I dance onto a new page

fresh and unstained

full of all the wisdom from the year before.

Blessed are the trials

that shape me for courage

and blessed is the Lord

who shapes me for love.

We can learn from the pain.

We can gather from the winter

which has taught us to grow

deep roots for the cold.

Warmth and grief can both

live in this body.

I will grow from both.

Here we are

here we go

leaping into what comes next.

Letters to God: I.

You fill the empty crevices

life has punctured into my heart.

You, light, spills through

pours in so much warmth

I find I am full.

My cup overflowing

my soul singing

taking flight to the sky.

Mystery

In the oceanic blueness

in the confidence of the roaring waves,

in the oneness where

earth meets sky,

water and air,

there is truth,

like lingering love

or ancient stones,

cold and silent,

bearing the seasons in isolation.

Are there answers in the silence?

In lost thoughts

falling like

fat sleepy drops of rain,

like distant train wheels

in twinkling lights.

There's too much fog in my head,

metal clanging around

like silverware dropping to the floor

or shattered plates spread out

like fragments of things,

of half-ideas,

of dreams,

of anything but quiet.

I cannot find the calmness of the ocean,

the sea-foam sprayed breeze

that is good and wise simply by being,

like those tall oak trees in the forest.

I cannot find the silence,

those dusty novels in the corner of the bookstore

or works of art that speak simply by being.

I am not an easy breath.

I am a raging thing

trying to be still,

to stop the spinning wheels in my head.

How can I contain all that is in me?

I watch the ocean rage and rise

crashing and quieting

both passionately and peacefully,

thinking that the heart is most like the sea

a mystery that never seemed to answer me.

Waiting to Bloom

It's a tough thing

trying to figure out your place

in the world,

your purpose.

You've got dreams,

goals,

but don't know how to get from A to B.

You see the final product,

but not the details.

Where do you belong?

You are young

and there are so many choices,

and it is terrifying.

You're like a flower left out in the dark,

dreaming of the sun,

waiting to bloom.

The Rain

The rain begins gently

trickling on the roof

gliding down the windowpane.

It's soft beating a drowsy lullaby.

Rainy days are perfect for

coffee and books and lost thoughts

that unfold from their box

and spread in your head like

the ripples of a stone

hitting water.

The water washes everything clean,

landing on the forest green leaves,

the translucent pond reflecting

the motion of life back to its woods

the swift deer running for shelter,

its hooves crunching the wet dirt,

a quiet echo through the forest.

Can it wash us clean, I wonder?

Cover us like slick newborns,

spill through all the cracks

where we are broken,

take away all the hurt

we've carried inside for so long.

The day fills with thoughts,

like would you let it clean you

or would you stick to your precious comfort,

listening to its soft pitter patter

from the safety of inside

because change is too painful?

I wonder,

have you ever dared to pray?

The Hourglass

Gazing at the hourglass

the hours pass by

tick tock into evening into tomorrow

catching and flying

a blur of blended days

falling through the hourglass

like sifting through sand.

Why the stillness and what can I learn from it?

Everything is a fragment of what once was

and what will be.

Among the sea and bells

earth and green

time and space

is the mystery of it all.

Some things cannot be known.

Some things require trust.

I step out under the sky

and release the burden with a breath.

Simply you and I out here God,

simply you and I.

Coffee and Poetry

A big cup of ideas

of rebirth

of words

swirling like

milk in a teacup,

thoughts brewing

in the cave of my mind,

silky and tangible,

strung together with

the magic tip of my pen.

Suspension

Here I am floating between two worlds

between dreams and reality

between wanting and waiting.

The foreign countries of my

heart and mind

grudgingly dancing this waltz,

hating and loving each other

all at once.

Black bird on a gray day

cutting through space

the wind lifting your wings higher.

Who will lift my wings higher,

who will give me wings to begin with?

If not you, than it must be I,

must be this young and old soul

must be these familiar bones

I call myself.

Here I am

flitting quietly through the world

still feeling I am getting nowhere,

standing still on the circus tightrope.

Should I jump?

Here I am,

still holding my breath.

The Beauty of the Day

Sick with worries

with thoughts

that spilled out of my mind

onto blank pages,

smearing

staining

them with words

with blood

with things never lost.

I stepped out of my head

and lay under the sun

until my pulse slowed,

until I was filled with color,

until my brain was silent.

The wind whispered to me

of the beauty of the day

and suddenly filled with calm,

I listened.

Night Thoughts

I was struck with the silence

of the night,

my wild thoughts blossoming,

pushing themselves towards

the front of my consciousness

plump with lost poems

sticky with all the words left unsaid,

skeletons sleeping within the walls,

a thousand butterflies taking flight

across the labyrinth of my mind.

The Seed of My Sorrow

I stood beneath the sad sky,

small and human.

I held my heart

in my hands

beneath the white moon,

bare and trembling,

rooted in place

like a tree planted

in the ground.

The shadow of a star,

I let my pain take flight,

become a wing

and leave me.

I died a hundred deaths that evening

and wept in relief,

crystallized drops

of the fountain of my emotion.

I let myself go

in the haunting twilight,

hazy and blue,

a half-light of

things lost,

and bled

for the last time

from the seed of

my sorrow.

Letters to God: II.

I think of you in the wake

of the milk-faced moon,

the lily flowers blooming

in eloquent shades of delight,

the soft rain breathing life

and bleeding deep green upon the land.

In the wave of your hand,

the gift of your presence

is an ocean wave of calm,

of encouragement.

I can bear anything

with you in my heart.

Lessons

Wet was the light

the damp green earth glistening

the dirt sinking beneath shoes

slushy, muddy, liquid

the aftermath of a ritualistic cleansing.

Still, the flowers are singing

gulping silky water

into their bodies,

teaching us in order to bloom

we have to experience the rain first.

Monday

Buried beneath the piles

of endless thoughts

cluttered worries

and hand washing,

I press pause

and breathe deep.

It's too crowded in there

in the mind that jumps

from topic to topic

and never lets me catch my breath.

Today today

we begin again.

Start the tea kettle

take a break

from the work that cries essential

and revel in the honey

in the sweetness of

this exhale

in the hope of a new day

in the heart that still stands

beating through it all.

Silent God

I find you in the stillness.

There among the rustling trees

the blue sky stretched wide

the green earth beating vibrantly.

Deep breath in

Deep breath out,

letting it all in

letting it all out.

There you are

silent God

speaking to me with no words.

There in the heartbeat in my chest

there in the hope in my soul

there in the wings of courage

you've taught me.

You take the shadows,

the messy pieces

and mold them with love,

placing them in my lungs

so I remember how to breathe.

You breathe life into dusty bones

that sprout and grow and cry with gratitude.

I couldn't see it then,

that your best work is always in the dark

when there's nothing to rest on but trust.

Resurrection power from seed to bloom.

It is when you most seem silent

that you're not.

The Best Version

Sown together

thread by thread,

thin strands of the

fiber of my being,

knitted back whole

like fragments of a scattered puzzle

finding their way back.

I have put myself back together

plunged through the dark cave,

dug and dug

with bleeding hands

to find the deepest part of me

that lay buried beneath.

I am not entirely done,

but I am learning.

I am a seed God planted

that must break down

to rise up fruitful.

I am slowly learning

the best version of who

I always had the potential to be.

Revival

The water falls through time

to the parched land within us.

Can this thirst be quenched?

Water that bends and curves

to the style of the race

among rocks and fallen leaves

and over my head

as I awaken with newborn newness

clinging to this bare version of me.

Among the wild and broken

the coming apart to mend

the torn cloth to healing

the restless to redemption.

I find it beating within a newly discovered strength.

Deep breath

from mouth to lungs to soul,

a revival.

I Come

I cling to you because I know

no other way than this:

your words tucked along

the pocket of my heart,

your light gleaming

through my soul

like a lamp in the fog.

Across the night sky

the stars scatter and make way

for the leading one to guide

the shepherds below

to a savior in flesh,

a promise in flesh.

I come too

with shaking hands.

I come to give you praise

I come to behold the Gift

I come to believe and be saved.

An Ode to the Potter

Mold me like clay O Potter.

You shape me with your hands

building me through every season.

Create in me a clean heart

that I may be a new creation,

that I may sing your praises.

Will I let myself flourish

or remain a scattered seed

stuck in bad soil?

Oh Lord,

teach me to do your will.

Take me deeper

into trust,

into truth.

Help me plant myself firmly

that I may know Your voice

among the chaos.

My Gardener, my Teacher,

my Hope in the wilderness,

I place all my faith in you.

Love

Purpose

Like lotus blossoms

floating downstream

your works are wondrous,

beautiful beyond compare.

Your love a golden burst of light

beating endlessly within my heart.

The hope of you sustains me.

Once a seed,

now a tree stretching its branches

higher into the sky

roots settled deep

within the proper soil.

You see

the foundation you set your life upon is

everything.

Oh the glory of your Presence!

I am weeping

laughing

singing

shaking

praising

with arms wide open.

You are a lamp guiding my path

my unsteady feet

and clumsy hands

reaching out to you.

There is power in Your name.

The earth beneath our feet

cries out *Holy Holy Holy.*

My God,

light of my soul

sun of my sky

wings of my heart,

I live to worship You.

The Root of Love

I am writing to tell you

I have discovered the root of love.

It began with God,

heaven and earth,

light and darkness,

day and night,

the waters divided by water.

It bled into the roots of the ground,

into the thick mud,

to the trunks of trees,

their branches spread out like fingers

reaching for the sky

with evergreen hope.

It spread to the ruby-throated hummingbird,

the green frog hopping onto the

purple and white water lilies,

the ripples from the jump

like silky bursts of movement.

To the silver-tongued fox,

the sweet and naïve deer,

the flock of geese by the blue lake,

to the cold morning in the mountains,

the crisp air that stings the lungs,

the white cotton of clouds,

the flowers blooming in color,

the sun kissing everything it touches,

to your lips from mine.

It is sweeter than red cherries,

peaches,

or pineapples combined.

It is the root of the root,

the master of the stars,

the truth of all we can hope to find.

God is in all of us,

in everything,

and so love is in all of us,

in everything.

Letters to God: III.

I find solace in your presence.

My constant companion,

the flower of my heart.

I rest all my hope in you.

Young Love

I want to read you like a book

turn page after page

get to know all your words,

trace over your thoughts

like lines on a map.

I want to sip you like a caramel latte,

all sweet

and milky

and awake,

stirred into a swirl

like watercolors before a painting.

You put the sun to shame,

all bright and golden,

star-like and dreamy.

You remind me of a Greek myth without the tragedy,

kind and hero-like,

a perfect dream.

The Shadow

In tender morning,

in rivers of fire and blood,

in quiet footsteps

ringing through the silence

like church bells

or a violin's song,

I have loved you.

Like droplets of rain

or tears,

I have cried out for you,

your name painted on my lips

like morning dew

on a petal.

I need only seek

the deep cave of my mind,

the working gear of

my thoughts,

like metal grinding

inside a clock,

and there you are.

.

The Awakening

My heart awakened like spring

at the sight of you,

the world in full blossom,

the gentle wind of love

attaching itself

and taking flight

within me,

a thousand butterflies

come to life.

Peaches

It was the evening of peaches

peach fuzz on your skin

fruit juice sliding down our arms

ripe peaches in our mouths

sweet and sweaty

the North Carolina heat

caressing us like lost lovers.

The sun tattooing us

with tender kisses

that left our orange skin

covered in that July glow.

We were young and hopeful

and wishing summer would last forever.

I told you I loved you

painting my heart with words

I would remember

for all the glistening

peach seasons to come.

Dig

The water laps gently,

the blue of the sky reflected

where we dance on the surface,

but sometimes I am afraid

to dip below,

to take you deeper.

Will we sink or drown?

Am I overthinking this?

We sit on the ground

but I am afraid

to plow into the dirt

with my bare hands,

to pull out the stems and veins

until I reach the roots,

afraid you will find them

dark and ugly and stained.

But the birds are singing

and the sun is out

like a spoonful of something

sweet and trustworthy,

and taking a leap

off a cliff,

out of my body,

out of my heart,

I begin to dig.

Taking Wing

The words fled me

like birds in the night,

silent and aching,

clusters of white petals

among the red land

of my heart.

Among the garden

of the world

of the sea

bells

prairies

trains

stars

earth,

my truth hid

in plain sight

laying at your feet

in quiet grace.

I opened my mouth

and a flower emerged

whispering in a honey voice

of all the things

it had been dying to confess.

My love slipped

out of my chest

and tumbled into

your arms like

a coconut falling

from a tree,

ripe and honest,

and the words

finally came to me,

taking wing from my lips.

A Star

Over and over again

teach me the language of love

of flowers and tears

longing and sunlight

music and memories

skin on fire by the moonlight.

I drank your face in from the cup of my hands

my belly rich with the taste of you.

Falling deeper

again and again

among the silence of time.

Life at first a stone

and then a star.

The Heart of the Night

Your name falls

into the heart

of the night

like a raindrop dripping

from a flower,

a soft word

ringing through the silence,

a ticking wristwatch,

a bell announcing

the hour you

cut across my existence

like the mouth of a kiss

landing in surprise,

stealing all my breath.

Two Drops of Water

It's gray and rainy outside.

The wind is cold,

but the coffee is hot.

It reminds me of Saturday afternoons

with my daddy.

Cold afternoons spent inside,

warm in my sweater and Starbucks mocha,

listening to the rain rage outside,

the smell of stacked pages and caramel in the air.

There's a quiet hum in the bookstore,

the rumble of low voices in conversation.

Daddy sits across from me with his square glasses,

barely any traces of silver in his dark hair for his age,

reading *Einstein and the Rabbi*,

and I'm flipping through a new thriller,

my brain spinning on happy fast wheels.

These little father-daughter dates are everything to me.

Applebees, next on the list.

A burger, vanilla milkshake, and laughter.

Then we head to the movies.

Films and books are our things.

Somos como dos gotas de agua,

you'd say.

Two identical drops of water,

falling in unison,

joined at the hip like

Peter Pan and his shadow.

The rain drips off the windowsill outside

and my heart swells,

wondering where my twin drop is today.

Revolution

At times I am struck

with the hand of grief.

Autumn falls from my heart.

Everything leaves,

everything changes.

The yellow leaf turns me gold

touches me

and I wither,

fall away.

I change,

rebirth brews in my soul.

With all the empty space

the void of my sorrow

the way I cling to things lost,

you love me still.

With a kiss to the forehead

like the tumble of green earth

kissed by the sun,

you take me as I am.

The revolution inside

the shift of mindset

the growth is necessary

to find me,

to find you.

You plant the seed of love God

and together we watch

as I begin to bloom.

The Vine

You are the true vine.

Teach me hem me prune me

that I may be fruitful.

Uproot me and root me again

and again and again

that I may grow deep

from good soil

and sprout and climb out

with new understanding.

Home

My husband is a tumble of earth

grounded and strong,

bubbling with kindness.

His arms are honey gold

dipped in a cup of sunlight

like wheat or sunflowers,

keeping me warm in their embrace.

I am lost in thoughts

that swirl like milk in a teacup,

thick as fog

heavy and restless,

a poet riddled with endless words

that pour out like

rain from the sky.

Together we will build and build

within the four walls of our home

within the four walls of our hearts

our differences completing what the other lacks

until we are unsure where one ends

and the other begins.

Autumnal Love

All my words

are in your mouth,

your eyelashes

like thick umbrellas,

shielding those pools

that watch me like

art in a museum,

studying every subtle line,

every hidden meaning.

I gave you my heart

under the autumnal moon,

a red secret unfolded

beneath the night sky.

Our roots intertwined

at the shore of love.

You whispered,

"you've got to waste away

with me now,

you're in my blood."

Poems

You,

delicately laced beauties

handwritten in thick ink

boats sailing toward the horizon

little islands unto themselves

sprouting with fruits

and all things green.

You pour out of me

and flourish.

Little flowers on pages

little whispers of triumph

little silver bursts of dreams.

I gather you in my arms and smile.

Saturday Mornings

In the slow rhythms of morning

the soft light stumbling into the room

the smell of warm sheets

and skin shaking off sleep,

your face, oh that face,

burns in my heart

like the gentlest flame

like a photograph pressed between

the pages of a book.

It is a candle on cold nights

a comfort on days

when the world is too much,

a lamp in the dark.

Your face,

I see it with open eyes

I see it with closed eyes.

Even when I sleep,

even when all else

has fallen away.

The Words

You will find yourself

dancing in every line,

every sentence structured

like the starry eyes I give you,

every verse a pining confession.

In a sea of words,

you are all my words.

One Spring Day

The day opened before me

like a flower,

like a flourishing bud,

sprouting and growing,

turning more wonderful

as the hours went by.

The grass like

thick silk

like soft blades

in the wind,

the trees swaying

to the music of the birds,

the sunlight landing on earth

like a tumble of gold

and us among the beauty of it all,

encircled in the one another's arms,

in love with spring

and each other.

The Bells of Love

If you were to listen to my heart

by the sea,

you would hear the

thrashing of waves

like the bells of love,

the melancholic

low string of a violin,

the soft wheels of infinite motion

like train wheels grinding in the silence.

The heart is like an overflowing river

with lightning storms

and flowers

and arrows of desire

and blood.

If you were to listen to my heart

in the gentle breeze,

your name would vanish into the wind

and my secret would pour out

like a lullaby

or the rain,

softly, and all at once.

A Discovery

In the shadow of the sun

my lips find yours.

Summer wind and warmth

a discovery sweeter than honey,

the day cut into slices like fruit

red moments stained in hunger

for a bite of something new.

In the cloudless evening blue

there was only me and you.

The Guide

I would like to be still now.

I would like to let the soft animal

pulse of my body grow silent.

Not speak for once- not speak at all-

let the quiet settle in my bones

and listen,

to the voice that speaks to my soul

to the voice that guides within.

A Prayer

Spirit of God

fall upon the open field

of my heart

fall on us

like morning dew

fresh upon a flower.

Fill a world

dry with thirst

hungry and aching,

for you are living water

in a parched, barren land.

Lead Me

Broken, barren

I come to you

a vast land longing to be filled.

The water falls from your cup to mine

overflowing, spilling.

Your mercy is a gentle flow

milk and seed

soft splendor blooming

breaking into new soil.

Where could I hide from your love?

Roots that stretch and wrap around you

cling to you

for you are a tree of life.

You are holy ground.

Lead me lead me lead me

in the way everlasting.

Sunlight

Beginning

I shake

and shed

the flower of

my sorrow,

ready for tomorrow.

I open my palm

and let the seeds

fly into the wind,

hopeful for a

new beginning.

365

A yellow sun burns through the days

burns through the scribbled notebook

the pages filled with thoughts

unfolding, laid down

sprawled across the silky white

in black liquid.

Red dawn, silver moon, starry sky

days, moments, blended

365

and here we are

diving into the new

into the fresh water

with our breaths held,

our hopeful hearts.

Good Morning

My sleepy bones

stretch and groan.

I am not through with dreaming,

but the night is through with me

and the day embraces me

like an old treasured friend,

wrapping me in its light,

the sun kissing my eyelids open.

I shed my drowsy petals

and look upon the green earth,

which is a fruit that the sky bites.

I am struck with the infinite beauty

of the life around me

and am filled with joy

that opens its mouth like a song,

painting my face with a smile.

Stains

Every poet holds within them

uncontainable emotions that overflow

and pour out from their hands.

Thoughts glide like the river

and take shape in the moonlight,

silky strands of water

dripping like your heart

confessing its secrets

in the night

by the sword of your pen,

a flaming arrow shooting words

into the sky.

We the artists squeeze

the juice of life

into our palms,

sticky and sweet.

We write and write and write

bleeding onto blank pages,

staining you with our stories.

A New Year

Moments painted on a canvas

sprinkled across a time lapse of the year,

days laced in sunrises and moon milk

running right into each other

one after the next.

This season ends

and a new one begins,

unfurls in God's palm

as we enter a new stage set

with the same characters.

I wonder what happens next.

My silk heart undresses its winter coats

choosing to be an open heart

ready for new things to come.

One Day in April

The wind stirred

the day awake,

the trees chattering

amongst themselves,

swaying in full conversation,

and I sat with my pen

listening,

ripe with thoughts,

ripe with poems.

Wildflowers

Wildflowers grow where they please,

in unexpected corners,

between cracks in the sidewalk,

in beautiful random places.

They are tiny and brave,

swaying in the wind,

but never letting themselves be blown away.

If they have the courage,

surely you can too.

Song of my Soul

I take a bite out of the day

like a cookie too sweet to pass,

the gold of the wheat

as the gold of the sun,

as the gold of my heart,

drinking the blue of the sky

as the blue of the water,

painting me in color.

The wisp of clouds lined up

like balls of cotton scattered

across the celestial plain,

the infinite land of the heavens.

It is a vast dream,

the day,

the kind that stains your spirit

and leaves you longing

for the warmth of its kiss.

Spring lands in the green fields

and the earth awakens,

awakening within me

the song of my soul.

Letters to God: IV.

Open palms

bleeding heart

lowered head.

I love and I love and I love

I praise and I praise and I praise.

I will not stop

for you are worthy

for you are worthy.

A Perfect Day to Write

I am entranced by the day.

The sun's golden rays

kiss the crown of my head,

the sky opening its mouth

like the waves of the sea,

like the bud of a flower

opening its petals to you.

It is a day to be reflective

and enjoys the smallest moments,

let your string of thoughts fall out

like a thread of water

being pulled out by a wand.

It is a day to create.

I pull out my pen

and drip words

as real and as wet

as the ink stains on my palms,

birthing life to the stories inside.

Comfort

There is comfort in the ocean,

the rise and fall of the waves,

always teasing the shoreline with a kiss

and promising to come back soon.

There is comfort in the salt air,

in the inhale and the exhale,

letting you clear your mind

from the scattered fragments

dancing around in your head

like paper cranes in the wind,

letting you breathe freely.

There is comfort in the sand,

in every individual particle clinging to your toes,

making you remember that God is an architect,

and though the world may be tough,

to stay soft to see

the beauty in simple things.

Let where you find comfort

cling to your heart like bees cling to honey

in the summer light

The Autumn Day Is

The autumn day is gray

and reeks of coming rain.

The deep red

the pale gold

the suitcase brown

the vivid green,

colors that fill the sight.

The wind blows and blows

stirring up the trees

the grass

the leaves

dancing in the air.

The spirit of nature

rises and rises

starting over.

How beautiful it all is.

Let it all in with

eyes wide open.

Breathe deep,

let's begin again.

A Seed Sowed

It plants itself

taking root

settling in

slowly, at first, then spreading

gaining speed as it moves

through the body

through the heart

through the soul.

Opening its wings like

a bird preparing for flight.

It lingers in the stem.

Built on a solid foundation,

it will not sway with the wind.

The unmistakable birth

of something deep and concrete

forming inside of me.

Once a seed I sowed

now flourishing magnificently

before our very eyes.

My faith.

Morning

Every morning the

world is reborn.

The earth stretches and yawns,

full of thistles and thyme

in its pocket.

A kiss for you,

a kiss for me,

sunlit and bright.

Shake off yesterday's weight

like shedding leaves in autumn.

Today is brand new,

a golden chance to be

who you've always wanted.

Listen to the wind chimes

chattering in the breeze,

twinkling laughter like

stars twinkling in the night.

You have the courage,

you have the strength,

you have the heart.

There is a love in nature,

the constant changing of seasons,

the fish constantly swimming to hope,

the sun constantly kissing

everything it touches.

There is love in you too,

in the snow-arched mountain of your back,

in the pine-needled mess of your hair,

in the red tulip of your lips.

Mornings are for reflection,

the soft blush of appreciation,

the earth-toned shade of thankfulness.

This morning,

you are awake,

you are alive,

and you will be just fine.

Italy

The cobble stoned path is bumpy,

the streets narrow,

the white-washed buildings

smelling of lavender

and heat from the market.

The voices around me merge

like bees bustling around

their Queen's nest,

a touch of grazie

and buen gorno

here and there.

The meaty man at the corner

barks for anyone nearby to buy his fish,

the low rumble of laughter in his belly

threatening to come out

when a tourist jumps at his voice.

The ladies in the handbag shop

gossip in husky tones,

like dark dry wine after dinner,

one of them stepping out for a cigarette,

red lips staining where her mouth touches.

My friends eat gelato happily

and I am soaking in the sunshine,

the honey flow of a different language,

the full-bodied aromas,

hitting me all at once

like an epiphany

or first love.

I am thinking

I want to travel

for the rest of my life.

Sticky Fruit

The wind skitters through the trees

rustling the leaves like

a wind chime song,

the sunlight drawing circles on my skin.

The days are all yellow and free,

smoky scents and juice

dripping down my chin,

biting into ripe fruit

in my sticky hands.

However you slice and dice it,

cut it up in little neat corners,

fold it nicely in half

for safekeeping in your pocket,

you cannot have it back.

An adult in revolt

reminiscing the nostalgia of childhood.

The days were honey and sweet

fruits melting in our mouths,

little schnauzer barking in the backyard

daddy grilling, the smell of meat

mom's laughter floating in the wind

kids running around in the sun

limbs stretching from one day

to the next.

The world shone in

bright hues of innocence

making wishes on eyelashes

games wrapped in a cloth of pretend

fighting and playing and eating–

simple.

Some sunny days

when the wind blows my way,

the memory of our summer shrieks

fill my ears.

I can still smell

sticky fruit in the heat.

Coffee Shop

The hum of voices washes over me

like a distant thing

or a drowsy dream,

far away and unable to touch me.

I sip my hot latte,

the sweetness clinging

to the insides of my teeth and lips,

like a warm feeling

lingering in the pool of your stomach.

I am lost in heavy layered thoughts

that when peeled back

reveal more thoughts underneath,

like peeling ripe fruit

and finding pieces of its coat

in your fingernails.

I find writing in a coffee shop romantic.

All the different

conversations lives connections

measured through cups of coffee.

The world screaming in color

and me in the midst of the motion,

tracking it all down with a notebook

and smooth-felted pen,

creating words with velvet liquid.

Really, I am writing a poem about

finding inspiration and studying

the things around me.

I am falling in love

with all the words.

Dripping them out of my fingertips

like silky water in the moonlight,

seeing them even when I sleep,

even when I wake.

Solitude

The sunlight pries apart the leaves

flashes of light slipping through,

little slits of golden glory.

I walk through the park

with a book in hand

ready to jump into a new story-

tales of sword-fighting pirates,

gothic Victorian dramas,

murder crimes in the twenty-first century,

forbidden romance in a Spanish country.

I am ready to immerse myself in

intricate plots, twists and turns

in the dazzling art

of words strung together

like Christmas lights spread out across a room.

There is something so real about reading outside

about hearing the orchestra of life

surrounding you like a thick fog,

all awake and chirping with joy and simply being.

I admire the day,

its bright coat of movement,

the flowers drinking up honeyed light,

the little bird sitting on

the branch of a bush,

studying his surroundings as I study him.

Do not disturb me today,

I mentally ask of the world.

Live in my absence as if

it were a physical thing,

a building with coffee stained tables,

and thoughts written on the walls.

Do not ask for me today

for you will not find me.

I am too much enjoying my solitude,

inhaling the simply joy

of being alone.

The Gospel

The word is near you

it lingers there in your mouth,

it dangles there on your tongue,

it longs to shout from your lips,

to burst into the sky

into the earth

into human minds,

to tumble into

every flower

every skeptic

every soul.

It is in your mouth

and in your heart,

dancing swimming longing to escape

to be shared.

For it is with your heart

that you believe

and with your mouth

you will be saved

by speaking the words

you were born to say.

Madness

The blue sky spread like a silk canopy over me

wisps of white clouds darting here and there

as I ponder and ponder.

I think of the madness of men.

Government's swimming in corruption

countries starving their own people

the foreigner running for sanctuary,

the wild beasts running deeper into the forest

until there's no more forest left,

the trees ripped from the root.

When did we forget decency?

It runs deeper than you would imagine

including the small and voiceless.

Sometimes it is all overwhelming.

The world continued in its ways

bowing to their false gods

Vanity, Greed, and Pride.

Silent hands drawn together

head bowed with hope fluttering

in this gentle prayer.

Cover this land with your gentleness

bring us back to the root of creation

to the love that laces everything,

let your glory and peace fill the earth.

Can we truly love our neighbor?

The simplest things seem the most difficult.

Have you become consumed by fear

that someone will take what was never yours?

Have you gone crazy for material things,

filling yourself up with what will never make you full?

If so, hungry you are and hungry you will remain.

Have you also gone mad?

Sleepy

Today the day is

drowsy and gray,

those thoughts once swept away

with the tide

now returning to fill my head

with nonsense.

I am a writer,

worse a poet,

therefore I am bound to sleepless nights

of stringing together words,

creating silver-spun tales

out of melancholy and dreams.

The day has barely begun,

but it is sleepy and slow,

the muted sky careless for my urge to nap.

I force myself to step outside,

scattered hair and scattered musings,

all my words gone,

all my words gently laid out

on a wooden desk with inky pen last night,

all my words softly sleeping

in the half-moon circles

under my eyes.

Poetry

The earth fills the day

with light

flowers

shadows

moths

branches

rivers

and sets everything on fire

in bursts of unfiltered beauty.

Poetry took form in the moonlight

slivers of silver and melancholy

lavender plants and clean air

the mountains and valleys of the heart,

the oceans, cities, sunlight.

I looked upon the scattered stars

and was moved by nothing,

and everything

all at once.

The words took shape

at the ends of my fingertips,

my heart broke loose with the wind.

Have You Called Your Mother Today?

They say it begins

with a soft voice

like a drop of honey,

a gentle melody

that you carry inside

and becomes the voice

in the back of your head.

When I think back on childhood,

it is my mother's voice

I remember best.

It was the sound of medicine and safety

the promise that everything

was going to be okay.

Though she couldn't carry a tune,

her voice had a musical quality to it,

a milky ease which flowed

from her tongue to my ears to my heart

like flowing water or a flower in my hand.

The trouble is flowers wither and droop

feeling the weight of time.

It is the same with mothers.

We take and take and take

and we don't always give back,

and we don't always give time

though time is the thing we least have.

When they are faded and tired,

when they have given everything,

squeezed every ounce of their heart

like a lemon,

you will stand back in surprise

wondering who this ghost is

where your mother used to be.

Be careful what kind of gardener you are.

Be careful how you treat your flower

or one day when you are searching

for the honey voice of safety,

you will find it a stranger

or worse,

simply silent,

simply gone.

A Visit

The dogwood blooms in the corner,

the mossy stone rock stands coolly

by the bubbling river.

The white house with blue shutters

stands as if you were still twelve,

dreaming of the big world outside

stuck in complex suburbia

with its safety and secrets.

Each of us our own universe,

each of us a stone and a star.

Do not simply let life

make of you what it will–

not with the stars,

with your hands,

with your path forged

by your blood and heart,

tears and deeds.

Return to your hometown

and people will remember you.

"But I've changed, I've changed," you'll cry out

burning with experience and travel and a mind transformed.

But the air still smells of pine trees,

of grilled meat, laughter, grass, memories.

The abandoned building at the end of the road

still fills you with melancholy.

You have grown but

the you that has always been you

lingers beneath your collarbones,

in the depth of the root.

Is that so terrible?

And the day is a nostalgic silk

in your verses of honey and fire

and flowing poetry.

Unraveling

Unravel me

pull me apart

thread by thread

unweaving slowly.

In the stillness

I lay the burdens down

I unfold.

In this room cloaked by truth

that shines too bright to ignore,

I hand you my stories.

Memory stacked upon memory

pain and joy and fear and faith–

all I have been.

Have mercy on me son of David

and in your kindness

take my heart

make it new.

I find you here

in the quiet place

in the unraveling.

Exhale

(Inhale)

I desire to unwind

unfold and not be folded anywhere

spread out the crinkled paper

the words written in black ink

with what I don't even know.

(Exhale)

I say this:

Let me float away with the stream

close my eyes and feel the sun.

Let it all (all that is within me)

be honey and kindness.

Smooth out the corners

so bitterness and anger can't hide at sharp turns

and I am poured out gently.

Let my heart float outside of my body

let it run with the river

let it unravel in the wind,

leave me and return

that I may know what it is

to breathe.

The Birds

The birds announce the morning

in collective voices,

in excited chatter,

in honeyed tunes

emerging from the depths

of their chests,

a choir of songs

on love and hope.

Every day the sun will

rise and you will rise

with it.

You are still here,

I am still here.

It is a gift to die every night

and be reborn in light in the morning-

God's kiss like a

stamp on your forehead,

breathing life into your sleepy lungs.

It's no wonder the birds weep with joy

and sing.

Pruning

Prune me

pluck away what does not serve me.

Place me where I can grow

where my leaves may unfurl

and stretch,

where trust sprouts from the root.

I can see it now

your faithfulness in all

of the green.

May the seed produce fruits

may I bloom in faith

may I dwell in your Presence.

I will abide in You

for the roots are tethered deep

within my soul.

To Let Myself Go [II]

I had to let myself go.

I had to light the match

and burn all the bridges

of who I used to be

in order to become

who I was meant to be.

I had to shed and shed until

the raw and pink of my body

stood before God

and the sun and the sky.

It was in the wilderness

that I began to drop

the petals of shame,

of regret and loss

of self-righteousness and ego

of judgement and self-pity.

I let God seep into my bones.

I had to unravel

slowly

painfully

beautifully.

In every season

I had to stretch and sprout and grow

uncomfortable as it was

expanding expanding expanding

until I was blooming

a metamorphosis a journey a resurrection

body mind heart soul

the coming apart to come back whole

altogether new.

You see I had to let myself go

to find who I am.

About Atmosphere Press

Atmosphere Press is an independent, full-service publisher for excellent books in all genres and for all audiences. Learn more about what we do at atmospherepress.com.

We encourage you to check out some of Atmosphere's latest releases, which are available at Amazon.com and via order from your local bookstore:

About the Author

Kimberly Olivera Lainez has had poetry published in A.B. Baird's *My Still Waters* book anthology and *Harness Magazine*. She has a bachelor's degree in Mass Communications with a Journalism concentration and won a bronze Jose Marti Award for Outstanding National/International Business Article.

Kimberly is a poet, writer, and blogger based in North Carolina. She likes to explore topics of spirituality, growth, trauma, healing, nature, love, and the tumultuous highs and lows of life. She first started writing stories and poetry in elementary school and hasn't stopped since. She runs her own blog at kimberlyalysha.com. You'll often find her writing in a coffee shop, buying plants, and reading her Bible. She lives with her husband and three dogs. *To Let Myself Go* is her debut collection of poetry.

CPSIA information can be obtained
at www.ICGtesting.com
Printed in the USA
LVHW110011150821
695337LV00008B/853

9 781637 528105